TELL US WHAT WE ARE

John Clifford

BENT KEY Publishing

First published in Great Britain by Bent Key Publishing, 2023
Copyright © John Clifford, 2023
The moral right of the author has been asserted.

ISBN: 978-1-91-532028-5

Bent Key Publishing
Office 2, Unit 5
Palatine Industrial Estate
Causeway Avenue
Warrington
WA4 6QQ

bentkeypublishing.co.uk

Edited by Rebecca Kenny @ Bent Key
Cover art © Samantha Sanderson-Marshall @ SMASH Design and Illustration
smashdesigns.co.uk

Printed in the UK by Mixam Ltd.

Dad, this book is for you.

CONTENTS

TELL US WHAT WE ARE

DISTANT SWEETNESS

how does the sky look?

How does the sky look as you find this?
Blue, or pale pink to fading purple?
Or possibly aflush and rinsed
In darkened inks and indigo?

I hope that these words reach you
As the light begins to break
I hope that you look up
And have to squint, and feel the warmth
Of your sun brushed hair
As it kisses the top of your head

And if so, that you might close your eyes
As I am doing now,
And that we can be close to one another.

moon

She's watched us a while now,
Traced our growing webbed constellation glow
Through her first, everlasting night
Lonely, though not how is often presumed
A lighthouse keeper, solitary beacon,
Maintaining the mirror shine
Of her swinging lamp as she dances in
Reels through the spray of the waves

The first that Eve sang to
In her secret moments,
And always the confidant worthy of trust,
She will hear our last whispers
Before we go dark,
Leaving her to lure fishes
With long rendered echoes
And await her own dusk

A single rare coin growing dim
In the murk of the water.

ego

He is alone here.
A cracked temple at the water's edge
Only air and echo sparing hope
Of restoration for his crumbling,
Weather-beaten being

He cannot still fully bear the sight of his addiction,
So he comes and he goes, tense with temptation
An intensity of ego pillared at the centre of his soul,
He pillories himself for it, before inexorably reconvening

A council of two meeting equal beauties,
Reverend in situ, held still
Until the winds wave one-half away
At a loss for adoration
With a rising shame riding on the ripples

He gathers wet pebbles from the water's edge,
Roughs the surface with enraged tantrums
Until Atmos sighs acquiescence again,
Enables him to turn bright, bloodshot eyes
To the caged mirror image of his deliverance

He drinks, hungry and deep
Until sick with himself
So the cycle repeats
Swan dive spiralling feast
Feeding the famine
Of the starved and disgusted,
Repressive. Self-obsessive.

He thinks, before long
He will see himself drowning,
And weeps.

spring draughts

Mix a sloe tincture
Drink to Brigid and the Imbolc
Every bit be imbibed
And bring abiding blossoms
In a measured unfolding of cherished treasures
A gold rush of seconds
Awash in the blackthorn
Glints against darkness

Exchanged for lazy mornings
Ones where the sun cannot
Fully prise the blinds open
And so lays, glowing
Rolling, lolling dog tongue
Beams against the bedsheets
Which trace their lines
Like sleeping fingers
Finding mine.

Such sickly liquor —
Grant me a fraction
Of the sweetness with which you overflow
Older than the comfort of half heard hour chimes,
Vague crackling wax wicks
And clepsydra pooled waters
With reflections on stars

A gift of rare grain and brief sparkle —
The meekness of living,
With a fortune of moments.

FINDING OUR WAY

To Memories Made In This City

We'll listen for the carillons of birds
They sound from the stone and slates
In the quiet twilit hour of the dove,
When the light still coolly bathes our avenues
And mocks the street lamps,
Ringing them like bells.

Before the sky is wrapped in dyed indigos
And laid to rest, we'll find each other slowly,
Let the seconds sift by like fine white sands
And in their final slipping grasp, etch each other
Into the surrounding tower blocks

Every spire we share is a stronghold
Hemming us in, keeping us safe,
Their columns the final pastel bastions
Crumbling to-night

I would rather we could lose ourselves
To this silver moment
Even now I turn it over
With these ruined hands which you once used
To trace the uneven fork tines of the skyline

It marks me so deeply that years from now
I fear I'll still be picking dust from deep beneath my nails
Until then I will drink the dregs
Of argent lustre from the memory,
Press it failingly to long reams of paper,
And tarnish it with inks.

Recovery

If I could return to
Those gloomy, dripping evenings
To see him once more
Clouded through thought and cigarette smoke
Laughing in his explosive fashion
I would want to rush forward
And bottle the air
To be opened on future occasions
Sipped and savoured like a fine wine.

Oh, to be drunk again.

Ghosts

We found tragedies and joys,
They came together, equal measures
Of times that we could walk and dance
In our old imagined avenues.

They came together in equal measure,
The silhouettes of what we were
In old imagined avenues
Together now they fade and blur.

The silhouettes of what we were,
Entangled webs of memory
Together now, they fade and blur,
Conjoined eternal reverie.

Entangled webs of memories,
The focus of them nearly lost
Conjoined, eternal reveries
That haunt the avenues at dusk.

Their focus now is nearly lost,
Eternally they will remain,
They haunt the avenues at dusk
To never see sunlight again.

Eternally we will remain,
I cannot tell you where we are,
To never see sunlight again
And lose the love of moon and star.

I cannot tell you where we are,
Oh love, do not let go of me
I cannot lose you, guiding star
To sink beneath abyssal seas.

Oh love, do not let go of me,
There is no light to set us free
We sink beneath abyssal sea
Entangled joy and tragedy.

There is no light to set us free,
We will remain eternally
Entangled joys and tragedies
My love, do not let go of me.

No one can tell us what we are.

Black Hole

There is nothing I can say
For you to hear,
No gifts that I can bring
Which won't be aptly torn asunder,

So let's agree we'll keep a fair distance,
And each go on,
Silently fucking things up
In our own special ways.

Silence

Few things sit more sour
Than the silence of a slammed door.
I hate the racket of that quiet,
What it crystallizes,
How it leaves you,
Unendurable and fearful,
And worse than when you started.

The stillness has tossed
My body like a crash before,
Left me hanging off the earth
For that awful second
Before the whole world
Rushes through to drown you
With a tranquil sort of violence.

LOSING EACH OTHER

Here's What I Remember:

The trill of the swifts
Honed along the grain of night
Cutting mourning songs

A Slow Ending

Clouds are faded
Pastel lines across the long horizon
Bricks settle in a block print
Of stamp-neat terracotta
Tiled to match their rooftops

Flitting sparrows flock in silent silhouette
And practice their calligraphy
Perched on the evening
Parakeets paint the air blue
Berating their neighbours
With borrowed admonishments

Amongst all this
The cold hollows out the air like absence
Burning my hands
And hanging droplets off my lashes

Or perhaps they are reversed
These famished things
Perhaps the same
And I'm confused
I find it hard to say
A thin veil hangs
A shadow over everything

05.06.22

It approaches
We will lift and lay you
Close beside your mother
Rest, now gentle
Soul against the earth
Leave a hollow in the rib crook
For a greater place of comfort

When we depart
We will not find you here again
Only where you have always been,
Visiting,
In other quiet ways;

Where I sit I see you now — a robin
Is gathering leaf and twig,
Assiduously building a nest in your palm,
Halting in its flitting.

I wonder.

If I remain quiet
On the stones which you maintained,
By the turf you set,
Beneath the shade of trees
Your warm hands formed and watered,
Would you stay a little longer?
Could you hold me, still?

Pink, Like Your Brain

Things can grow grim in here.
The rot sneaks in to hide in quiet corners,
And whispers its taunts
Through grime caked lips

It's too easy to listen for it,
Let shoulders fall and accept the murmurings
When they come from a place of comfort,
To sit and look at your yellowing insides
And concede them for who you are.

But they are not the same, the rot and you,
And little truly good is gained in ease,
So strive to clear those calcifying colours;
Take the time to care, and scrub your insides
It may leave you fresh, and pink, and raw,
But in due course I promise you'll feel better for it.

RETURNING
UNFAMILIAR

Home Town

My warren of streets
Has been filled and re-dug.

The net it casts still keeps its familiar points:
Bus stops, building site skeletons
Which were libraries once,
The ancient, flaking, friendly rust
Of the Dudden Hill line,
The baked-in pavement grime,
Which weathers every errant
Council funded power hose blast.

But the routes I took
Each endless week and quickening year,
Through which I wore
A teenage groove into the pavings,
Have all contorted with strange corners
And unfamiliar windings

There is no mark of me here —
It's as if these were just roads,
As if, in ways I never fathomed,
There is no path to take me home.

Leaning against station bricks,
Who know me at a second glance,
I scoff chips from an old greasy spoon gaff
That kept me fat in brighter days,
And consider my place.

The old fried fish hoardings are replaced
With shiny chromes and neon lights,
Though impressively the hands behind the counter
That scoop and season little miracles
Are not changed as yet.

In the dark, I follow a familiar vein of vinegar
And grin clouds into the lamp light.

At least the taste is still the same.

The Feral Parakeet

Far removed from an untouched sort of wilderness,
You sit draped in London's twilight finery
Cold air and mists, brightly buttoned with street lamps

You and your countrymen find different kinds of comfort,
And though your crests might share the same verdant hue,
Your calls resonate with a certain discordancy.

You're far from home, little bird,
Far from home and lost
In a Winter more frigid than your bones can remember

You bathe in duck ponds on the hill,
Puff out your chest and mimic the melodies
Of those better suited to this jigsaw piece city,
And call in their tones 'til you can't hear the difference

It does not matter.
Those feathers will still paint your unbelonging
Into the old English oak you roost in,
And it will ever grow in ignorance of you.

Burning Bright

Plucked and wrested from her prowling
Dug out from the fine mesh
The canopy cover, the fern and foliage
Upon which she had first been couched
Layered in a mussed outline
A vibrant blur unseen against the green
Her fur, now finely smoothed in indigo
Sharp cut, polished sheen and glimmer
From silent ferocity of the forest floor
She is unearthed, and made to dance
In the light, the precious gem
Gleaming, leaping from her setting
Broken amber, ever poised.

LIFELOCKED

Natural Light

These days I feel you through a prism.
The experience is uncomfortable;
Where usually you'd cast a fresher air in amber,
Here and now we simply heat our squalor
And extend this Summer squall

Far in fettle from all photosynthesising feeling,
I fear we're growing sick within each other,
Forming a malaise of heavy humours
In the glare and unusual reflections

I want to feel your warmth
Against me on the grass again,
To hear the long-curbed susurrus of the city
And take joy in our growth once more

I miss you in your current form;
Miss the burgeoning love we had
And everything before we were forced
To feel natural things in these unnatural ways

I hope in time you might meet me on the other side
And that we find ourselves again.

Parasitic

Remember how fast they were to clap.
Remember when they turn to vilify,
Declare us parasites, and slap aside
The careful hands that healed us.

Remember how a red-eyed sun,
Which swallows its discomfit now,
Elevates as angels those
It squealed and screamed to sack.

Crumple up and chuck the fucker
Who first welcomes, then disparages.
Do not let them take their snipings,
Fickle good immigrant narratives,
Hatred of the poor and weak,
And digs at those marked Other,
Gloss them over with another
Sneering thin veneer of thanks,
And laugh their pig-eyed,
Grasping, bigot heads off to the bank.

Do not press yourself to praise applause
That time to come leaves hollow.
Push instead, and fight to reparate
In finer days that follow;
Hold your place lest they erase
And redraw lines to suit their views.

And remember when we're out of it
Who truly feeds on who.

Vultures Over Haiti
after Eduardo Galeano

The winners need a loser
They can parade to all the runners up
There's no point to holding mountaintops
If no one else is climbing
So they say *Look.*

Look at the belittled,
Zero culture, no infrastructure,
Hut dwellers, poor fellas —
They live just across the pristine beaches
We plant our parasols in

They're selling their lives
Alongside knock-off football shirts
Holiday tat and generational hurt
Churned out for the winners

When our Antoinette-adjacent spending
Boils the sea and heaps hurricanes on homes
Mashing timber and limb
Water and death
In a meaningless madness
You needn't care for their passing
Caring has no currency

Though they face rebuilding obliteration
You'll see the borders we've sown in
Reforged chains are held intact

So make sure to stay on the side of us
The grass here is greener

Where soil is not oil slicked
They can clean it
After they are done
Mixing us one more
Resort bar rum cocktail

Designed for the imperious
Who socialise bankruptcies
Privatise profits
And make sure money
Is always freer than the people are.

Remembrance

Come kneel, and wash your red coats
In the fields where they are gathered,
Watch men who smell of oil burning
And some older staleness,
Dip their heavy, moustached heads
In puddles of a long-spilled gore,
To re-emerge with carmine blossoms
Clasped between their teeth.

They turn towards you in the dark,
And, to a heartbeat drumming, whisper
Come and join your brothers
Join your sisters, join us all,
Think of what a garden we could grow.

Do not give yourself unto
Their taut and pearly smiles,
Stare down at their grasping hands,
Still slickly warm and dripping,
And be sure not to trust them;

In times yet to follow, red will run
And fill those furrowed puddles fresh
And you will look then to those men
Each pallid, gaunt as carrion crows

And, staring at the carnage set to follow
You will know why
Storms which level cities
Are rewarded with a human name.

Pin that wound above your heart,
Remember for a moment,
But wonder not what words
Your monarch whispers to the Cenotaph.
Theirs is an over-practiced prayer
Which wears the stones when spoke aloud:

This harvest of another year
We offer here in wreath and shroud.
But you will not have long to wait;
We will be reaping soon again.

ACKNOWLEDGEMENTS

My thanks to Rebecca Kenny for the belief she's shown in me with this book, and to Bent Key for endlessly championing new writers and bringing so much joy to UK poetry.

Thank you to the Manchester and Leeds poetry communities for being welcoming, giving me the inspiration to listen and share, and just generally being too bloody talented.

To my friends, you're all dead fit. Sorry I'm so bad at replying to messages.

To Martha, for bringing me to poetry and keeping me sane while we wrote and while we didn't. Here's to the Escaprils we never finished.

To Sahir, for being my best friend and co-conspirator. I'm very happy we can harmonise each other's madness.

To my sisters, for being so artistically gifted that I had to write a book to not be left out. Together we're capable of anything except building a sphinx out of gingerbread.

To my mum, for being a brilliant example, always caring and nurturing our creativity. None of this would have happened without your love.

ABOUT THE AUTHOR

John Clifford is a queer writer and performer who has shared his stories at venues and events across the UK and US without anyone managing to stop him so far. Raised in London, he has lived in Manchester for more than a decade, writing about nature, identity, love, grief, and other dirty things.

His work has been performed in the Manchester Art Gallery with the Northern Poets Society, in musical collaboration with Open Collab as part of the 2022 Cheltenham Literature Festival, and was displayed in Manchester's Northern Quarter as part of sayin's city-wide National Poetry Day displays.

This is his first chapbook. He's very happy you're holding it.

Instagram: @jayceepoetry

ABOUT BENT KEY

It started with a key.

Bent Key is named after the bent front-door key that Rebecca Kenny found in her pocket after arriving home from hospital following her car crash. It is a symbol of change, new starts, risk and taking a chance on the unknown.

Bent Key is a micropublisher with ethics. We do not charge for submissions, we do not charge to publish and we make space for writers who may struggle to access traditional publishing houses, specifically writers who are neuro-divergent or otherwise marginalised. We never ask anyone to write for free, and we like to champion authentic voices.

All of our beautiful covers are designed by our graphic designer Sam at SMASH Design & Illustration, a graphic design company based in Southport, Merseyside.

Find us online:
bentkeypublishing.co.uk

Instagram & Facebook   @bentkeypublishing
Twitter   @bentkeypublish